The Adventures of Frakash in the Land of the Geekmeisters

Elen Ghulam

All characters and events in this book are fictional, and any resemblance to actual persons, living or dead is purely accidental.

Copyright © 2106 Elen Ghulam
All rights reserved.
ISBN: 0978187237
ISBN-13: 978-0-9781872-3-1

Frakash was a garden gnome who thought magic was boring. Other garden gnomes entertained themselves by turning hideous people into frogs or sending goblins at night under the beds of children who had exceeded their weekly tantrum quotas. To Frakash such pursuits seemed mind-numbing. Memorizing reams of magic spells to be recited at absurd moments was not Frakash's idea of fun. Like all his kin, Frakash owned a copy of *Mastering the Art of Mischief of Every Kind*, but his copy sat neglected on the shelf, the way a sundial sits in the backyard of a wristwatch owner. The entire clan of garden gnomes would consult with this mystical bible of pranks at night before diving into dream land. The following day they would explode into giggles after placing a fish behind a car's sun visor to watch the driver's expression when the stinky mess flopped into his lap. Another favorite act of impishness of the gnomes was to sneak up behind two people enjoying a lengthy conversation to tie their shoe laces to each other's. "How trivially silly", Frakash would murmur and shake his head with disapproval. Frakash was a wholly different kind of gnome, even the thought of crossing marshy bogs to charge defenseless dragons seemed futile to him. Whenever his gnome friends came to him suggesting a fair maiden rescue mission, his response was the same: "Why bother? Let the dragon keep his fair maiden …. Ayeeeeee! These princesses are so hard to please; the dragon deserves what is coming to him."

Although his friends thought him slothful, Frakash ignored them and occupied himself with gardening instead. He enjoyed planting tomatoes and tulips in unexpected places. The gardening occupied him, but didn't fulfill him. Most of the time, Frakash sat around sighing long and languished exhales. His soul ached for an exit of his fairy-tale existence. A mysterious longing grew into an insatiable volcano in his heart.

One beautiful sunny day, Frakash was weeding in a garden that always needed oodles of work. It was the garden that Laila liked to call Laila's garden, yet Frakash called the Heaps of Labor garden. Laila was the woman that lived in the house with the Heaps of Labor garden. Frakash would observe her when she sat on the sundeck, drinking a cup of coffee or working on her laptop. She was a quiet sort that rarely said anything but when she did, it was sharp as an axe. Laila was nothing like Frakash's gnome friends. She worked as a computer programmer in a software development company and would say words that Frakash didn't understand; like server, upload and database. Laila would sit outside for hours focused on her laptop, tapping on the keyboard with piercing attention. Every once in a while, her breathing would slow down, her body would stop moving and a fierce look would appear in her eyes. In those moments, Frakash wished he had a magical crystal to show him the thoughts forming inside Laila's head.

Laila's children would poke Frakash in the eyes. His eyes would be sore for days and Frakash would grow prickly. Even more irritating to Frakash was Laila's husband. He foolishly competed in his gardening work. That man was clueless, he would plant flower pulps in the shady side of the garden instead of the sunny side and pruned the shrubs with a light trim that hardly made a difference. "Why doesn't this man just quit trying?" Frakash would think to himself each time he was about to undo Laila's husband damage in the garden. Despite all the annoyances, Frakash enjoyed working in the Heaps of Labor garden because every once in a while he would hear something that tickled his imagination. One day, Frakash finished his work and decided that it was a good time for a sighing break. He sat underneath a purple shrub that seemed suitable for the pursuit and just when he was about to exhale, he overheard Laila talking with her husband.

A trace of sadness came in Laila's voice. "I love my work, but I feel a dark menace lurking underneath the surface." Laila paused hesitating and then looked straight into her husband's eyes and said, "Somebody among my co-workers .... Darling! Are you listening?.... is trying to sabotage me with doughnuts. It is as if an evil spell has been cast upon me. You know how hard I have been trying to lose weight in the last four months. Every few days, somebody brings free doughnuts to the office. I try to ignore them, but it is as if I am possessed by the sugar seduction fiend, I can't resist." Frakash overheard Laila complaining. "I can hear the greasy calorie bombs saying with an alluring voice: Come grab a doughnut and stuff it in your mouth."

Frakash's ears perked up as he heard a rumble coming out of Laila's stomach. Laila swiftly changed the subject. A joyfulness entered her voice. She bragged about her latest victory at work: "Yesterday, I presented my new design ideas to the team; the boss loved it and said that my design was the most brilliant design he had heard in months. Everybody else agreed. Even Mr. Grumpy Bumpy had to agree that my idea was alright. I am the queen of the geeks." Laila said to her husband with excitement. Frakash felt awestruck with what he heard. He decided to go to his hut to ponder the events of the day.

Unable to sleep, Frakash spent the whole night thinking: "Wow! Laila uses logic to solve problems at her job", Frakash marveled. "Instead of memorizing the same tired old list of magic spells that has been passed down the generations for thousands of years, Laila gets to come up with something new, something that she created all by herself." Frakash nearly stopped breathing in awe of Laila's work. He was tantalized by thoughts of presenting genius ideas to a group of geekmeisters. He fantasized about a meeting where he presented impressive ideas. As a reward the geekmeisters would bring him mouth watering doughnuts to feast on. He could imagine others looking at him with adoration admiring every word he uttered. To add to his brilliance, he could use his magical powers to break the evil spell cast upon Laila. He could see Laila looking at him in admiration and thanking him for the help. An irresistible urge to visit Laila's place of work overcame Frakash. He tried to convince himself that an adventure would not suit his temperament and that routine and sameness was the foundation rock of his being. Yet all night he dreamt about eating doughnuts and impressing the geekmeisters. The next day he tried to push those ideas out of his head, but a flood of yearning had been unleashed and Frakash was possessed by a single passion: to join the office of the geekmeisters and become a creative genius.

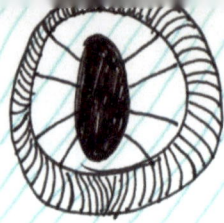

Bugoodle

To err is human.
To completly mess up,
takes a computer

That night Frakash used magic to sneak into Laila's backpack, the same backpack he saw her carry to work every day. In the morning, everything went according to his plan. As Laila walked past the large glass front door of her workplace, Frakash was riveted with a mixture of emotions that rumbled inside his body the way thunder reverberated in still air. The adventure had already started for Frakash and his heart was spinning like a twirling dervish. Laila, busy thinking about the next brilliant design, never opened her backpack in the morning and never suspected the stowaway garden refugee on her way to work. Frakash managed to get through the security without a problem. As soon as Laila walked through the large glass door, Frakash jumped out of the backpack and into the front hallway of the office of the geekmeisters. "Wow! I made it, I am here!", Frakash jumped up and down with excitement. As he looked around his new surroundings, he was awestruck by what he saw. The walls were perfectly white, not a single smudge or speck to be seen. The earth was covered with a plush fuzzy light blue material that was pleasant to touch; Frakash wished he could roll face down in it. Frakash reasoned he didn't even need to wear boots. Everything was clean; there was no dirt, no worms and no crawlies. The geekmeisters sat in perfectly shaped boxes, There was no noise, except for a faint sound of the efficient clicking on the keyboard in the background, which blended together into a harmonized buzz. There was no smell either, not of manure, not of dirt, not of anything. Frakash could feel

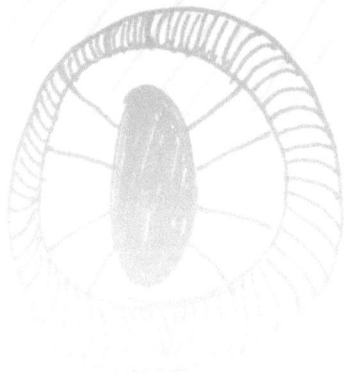

the relief in his sinuses as they smelled nothing for the very first time in their tired existence. "Oh

this place is heaven", Frakash thought to himself as he closed his eyes to soak up the moment.

Alas, Frakash's rapture came to a hasty end. Suddenly, out of nowhere a commanding voice descended upon him from above. "May I help you?" Frakash encountered the ever vigilant and always watchful office manager called Jenny. Frakash didn't know what to say. He muttered something about being a visitor. "Who are you visiting?" asked Jenny in a polite, yet firm voice. Despite her charming appearance, Jenny could be monstrous to an uninvited guest at the office. Frakash shrugged his shoulders and gave no answer. In no time, the stowaway garden refugee found himself being unceremoniously kicked out of the office.

Frakash was stricken with a thunder bolt of rage. He never felt such anger in any of his past gnome lives. Wishing he could lay flat on his stomach and pound his fists and feet on the ground like he saw Laila's children do sometimes, a dark shadow eclipsed his heart. "I belong with the geekmeisters, I want to be one of them", an inner voice rumbled through. "No giant glass door, no office manager and no security system can keep me out", he exclaimed to no one in particular. For the first time in his life, acts of mischief of a dark kind entered his fantasies; the kind that is forbidden even by the gnome essential book— *Mastering the Art of Mischief of Every Kind*. Frakash surprised himself with an impulsive act.

Frakash stood outside the giant glass door, observing geekmeisters walking in and out of the office. He noticed that they wore t-shirts with mysterious words printed on them. "Maybe my shirt gave me away", reasoned Frakash. "I need one of those geekmeister t-shirts!" Frakash followed the one whom the geekmeisters called James into the men's washroom. Once in there he cornered him, using his gardener muscles and three magical spells, Frakash forced James to take off his t-shirt. Convinced that if he was dressed like a geekmeisters nobody would suspect that he was a garden gnome. Frakash tied James' hands and feet and placed a

handkerchief around his mouth. Feverishly, Frakash ran out of the men's washroom and tail

gated one of the geekmeisters as he entered through the great glass door. The unsuspecting

geekmeister opened the door for Frakash using his security card and Frakash followed him into

the office. This time, Frakash knew not stand in the hallway looking mesmerized by the

antiseptically linear world. Hastily he ran into the first unoccupied perfectly shaped box.

Frakash looked at the computer sitting on the desk and felt thrilled to get a chance to try programming. "How hard can it be?" thought Frakash to himself. He began to stare intently at the screen the same way he had seen Laila do while sitting on her sundeck. There were many words on the screen that Frakash couldn't understand, but he maintained his intense gaze and squeezed his face muscles. After a while, he began to notice patterns in the words that appeared on the screen. Aghast, he discovered that the lines of code contained violent language that Frakash disapproved of. "If I rewrite this program using more life affirming words I might be able to change the life of the geekmeister who labors in this box", Frakash reckoned. He changed things around - "Trigger" became "Happy Event", "Alert" became "Joyful tid-bit" and "Kill Process" became "Whistle cheerfully while you wait". Frakash was quite amused, but after only a few minutes, the machine became angry and began making strange noises. The picture on the screen turned blue, like the sky. Frakash did not understand the meaning of the words: "System Error". Frightened, he fled a few meters away into a dark and deserted corner of the office.

Frakash came upon a large grey beast standing all alone. He figured this was the logic kingdom's dragon. Like everything else in this place, it came in straight lines and sharp angles. The grey dragon was making a menacing humming sound. Frakash was afraid that the beast might attack him. "Poor geekmeisters, they probably don't know how to deal with him" thought Frakash to himself. "After all, geekmeisters don't have time to take dragon charging training like garden gnomes do; I will thrash this beast into obedience in no time and impress all my yet to be friends" was Frakash's reckoning. Frakash began reciting the dragon submission chant: "Foooooooooooo, fooooooooooo,fooooo,fooo,foo, kafo!" and then charged forward with absolute certainty, to grab the dragon's scales around his eyes. The unexpected happened, the dragon began to shake and flash with blinding lights that didn't burn. Instead of spitting fire the dragon spat sheets of paper. Frakash froze with shock. He had heard of flying carpets, but never heard of flying papers. The paper piled on top of him and gave him tiny little cuts all over his body. Frakash was mortified that his dragon charging didn't work. Worse than that, his body was getting mutilated. With a genius spark the bush whacking spell came to him. "Ay-feeba-yuy, Ay-feeba-yuy, out of my way boom." Frakash recited quickly. His feet lifted off the floor and the papers slid of his body. "I am so glad some of the gnome magical spells still work here", Frakash felt hugely relieved to be free of the constricting paper. As soon as Frakash's feet touched the ground, he

began to run towards a sunny corner at the other end of the office.

Frakash's heart was banging against his chest the way an African drummer would strike his drum. A swift freight overtook him and he couldn't remember the tranquility spell from his book. Down the hallway next to a window, he saw a few potted plants. Frakash decided that if he would stand among the plants and imagine that he was in the Heaps of Labor garden sighing underneath his favorite shrub; it would help him lower the volume of the ruckus in his chest. Frakash stood between two majestic tall plants and closed his eyes, letting out three lively sighs. Ehhhhhhhhhhhhhhhh, Ehhhhhhhhhh, Ehhhhh. Frakash felt the rumpus in his body calming down. Out of nowhere, three monkeys dropped from the sky, jumped on Frakash and began scratching him. Frakash was so scared he thought he might jump out of his pants. He pushed, swatted and stomped until he managed to get the monkeys off his body. The monkeys sat on the floor dumbfounded and suddenly looked all cuddly. Frakash didn't understand why they attacked him out of the blue and then stopped for no reason. Nothing made sense to Frakash in this place. "I don't know what I am doing here?". Frakash felt desponded. "Even my boring magic spells don't always work in this world." That is when it hit Frakash, "I have been approaching everything the wrong way. Magic doesn't matter in this world, it is all about logic. I need to go through a magic deprivation phase, which will give my logical muscles a chance to develop." Frakash felt happy because he realized that he still had a chance to belong. Vowing not to use any magical spells, he walked down the hallway with confident steps, assured that his new attitude will

get him what his heart desired.

Frakash peeked into a meeting room. In there, he saw a group of tired geekmeisters working vigorously on perfecting a dizzying array of designs. They had stacks of documents in front of them and were drawing shapes and lines on the board with enthusiasm. Frakash joined them and began to listen in. Sitting on one of the beautiful and soft chairs made him feel important.

Frakash didn't understand what the geekmeisters were talking about. He tried to listen attentively and over time he gathered that the geekmeisters were talking about designing something called a Knowledge Base. It seemed to be a way to classify information so that computer programs can find the right kernel of information in a huge hay stack of it. The one that the geekmeisters called Mike got up to show his design ideas. To Frakash's amazement, Mike began to draw a design that mimicked trees. Although Frakash didn't understand everything in the diagram he understood trees, and understood the idea that a tree has branches and leafs. "Finally! Something that I know oodles about", delighted Frakash. "This is my chance to shine in the spot light". Frakash jumped up from his chair and onto the table and said what he was waiting to say all along "Listen up people; I know the perfect way to solve this problem". Everybody stopped talking and they all were staring at Frakash.

This was the first time that any of the geekmeisters noticed Frakash, for until then he was hidden under the table. They were all surprised to see somebody so short, wearing a long beard and a pointy hat. "Maybe he is a recent immigrant from a far away land with weird customs", thought Mike to himself. "Maybe he suffers from a genetic defect" thought Doug. "Maybe he has been recently divorced and the bad grooming is a symptom of his depression", thought Desiree. All three geekmeisters had completed their cultural diversity sensitivity training as mandated by their company. They had been coached on the perils of discrimination against anybody because of his/her culture, race, gender, physical appearance, class, educational background, manners or intelligence. Breaking the company's cultural diversity rules was punishable with dismissal. Since none of them wished to lose their job, all three geekmeisters acted as if seeing an 11 inch guy with a pointy hat standing on the table was perfectly ordinary.

Frakash proceeded to talk about his idea: "Trees are beautiful, they are tall, they are green and they provide shade, but ….. shrubs, although less visually impressive are far more useful. Shrubs are woody little trees that have a bazillion wild braches and with so many leaves that are too numerous to count. Plus they come in different colors, not just green. Their leaves don't fall and a good pruning always does them good." The geekmeisters eyes lit up. The one that the geekmeisters called Doug, got up and said "Aha! That is a brilliant idea, what the new guy is saying is that we need a structure that is more flexible than the standard tree design, yet resilient enough so that it can handle large mass of data, the shrub design. I think what the new guy meant was …". Doug got up from his chair and began to draw a group of designs that were marvelous. "Isn't this what you meant … new fellow, by the way what is your name?" Frakash introduced his name to the group and although he didn't understand most of what Doug drew on the white board, he claimed that the shrub design was his idea. The geekmeisters assumed that Frakash was a new employee, shook his hand, wished him luck in his new job and thanked him for his contribution to the meeting. Frakash achieved a tiny morsel of approval and sensed a feeling of belonging. Warm fuzzes were flowing through his blood and he could feel his cheeks burning.

Now super confident, Frakash peeked into the meeting room next door. There he found a group of geekmeisters playing a video game. Frakash was willing to take on another adventure. He grabbed one of the game consoles and moved the little knobs around. He realized that each time he moved a knob or pressed a button, something happened on the screen to a fictional character that he controlled.

The three geekmeisters sitting in the room were surprised to see an 11 inch being standing on the chair with a pointy hat.

"He must be a disgruntled programmer fixing the same bug for the tenth time", thought Ralf to himself. "O no! not another visit your parent at work day. Those kids are so annoying. Why is this kid wearing a fake beard?" thought Sam. "Great! They finally hired somebody who is even shorter and has more facial hair than me", mused Frank. All three had taken the cultural diversity sensitivity training as well and said nothing.

"O this is even more fun than drawing designs", thought Frakash. The objective of the game was to defeat as many enemies while collecting as much loot. To Frakash, this was familiar territory.

He was a professional loot hoarder by training as a garden gnome. Although he didn't know much about guns, he had good working knowledge of the bayonet. Frakash felt grateful for the first time in his life for the dragon charging training he received in gnome school. He remembered all the times he had told the other gnomes that it was a waste of time. Here he was putting it into good and constructive use for the first time. Although the game was fast paced and Frakash was not able to use any of his gnome battle spells because of his vow, in about an hour he defeated the most number of enemies and collected massive loot. All the other geekmeisters looked impressed with him. Sam gave Frakash a high five and said "Wow! Dude! You totally creamed them". Frakash felt happier than he had ever been. He felt that he was among those that understood him and were at his level. He was home.

Laila

Feeling happy as happy can be, Frakash decided to explore the office some more and walked into the stationary room. While looking at all the beautiful boxes he encountered two beings with sharp teeth that terrified him. Frakash had heard about vampires and werewolves, but wasn't sure if that is what he encountered in the stationary room. he prayed that he wouldn't get bitten by either creature because he had no desire to transform into anything other than a geekmeisters. He wanted to use a magical spell badly but didn't want to break his vow. He felt paralyzed without magic and didn't know what to do. Then he remembered something he read, about garlic keeping vampires away. So he ran out as fast as he could into the kitchen, hoping to find some to protect him.

In the kitchen, Frakash found a box full of doughnuts sitting on the counter. The dazzling sight made him forget all about garlic and vampires and presented him with a new dilemma..... which doughnut to eat? Each one was unique and special. Each one looked delectable and Frakash faced yet another state of paralysis. The paralysis of indecision was even harder to deal with than the paralysis of fear. After 20 minutes of trying to come up with a strategy to tackle the problem, Frakash closed his eyes and chose a random doughnut. Frakash raised the doughnut close to his lips, he could smell the sweetness in his nostrils. When the doughnut touched his lips, he could feel sugar grains rubbing gently against his taste buds. Frakash licked his lips, and then took a bite. The taste was hypnotic. The minute the doughnut left his mouth into his stomach; Frakash wanted another one and then another one and then another one. In a few minutes, Frakash surprised himself by eating the whole box of doughnuts. He fell on the counter into a food coma.

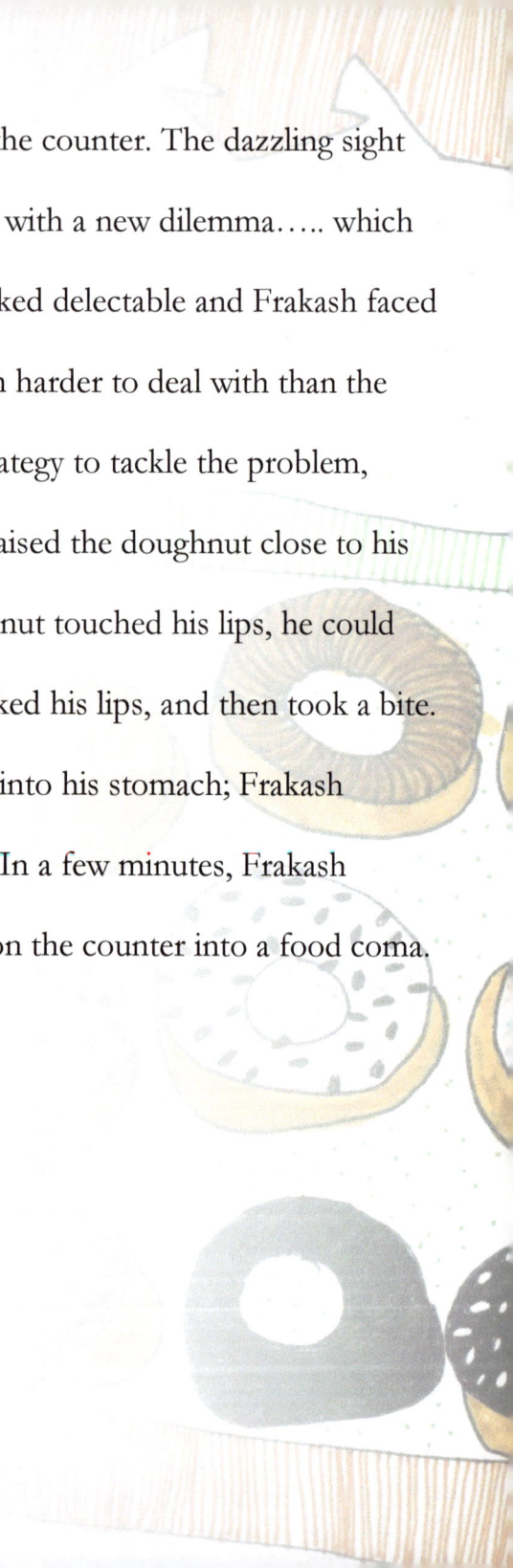

Frakash felt drowsy when he woke up from sleep. He was half in this world and half floating in a dream landscape. Frakash staggered out of the kitchen realizing that eating a whole box of doughnuts was a foolish idea. While walking in the hallway, he passed one of the perfect boxes where a geekmeisters was laboring. Frakash decided to observe from a distance and watch what a geekmeisters does at his computer, hoping that he might learn something. The geekmeisters typed the words "**ihath makes baba ganoush**" into a box on the computer screen and in a clickity click a video played. In the video, there was a woman hugging an eggplant. She looked serene but disturbed. Suddenly, a peacock showed up and began to stab the eggplant with a knife. Everything seemed strange yet normal. The woman in the video looked troubled but resigned, There was a pained smirk on her face. Frakash felt a rush of mysterious anxiety scuttle through his veins. He started to think that perhaps he was still dreaming. That is when he heard Laila screaming down the hallway. Frakash had never heard Laila scream before, yet he recognized her voice.

Frakash rushed towards the kafuffle to find James standing shirtless and looking angry. "Go back to the kingdom of landmines which is where you belong", yelled James at Laila. Without stopping to breathe, Laila yelled back: "You ignorant twit, I do not come from the kingdom that is now ravaged by landmines, I come from the kingdom that is ravaged by rooftop snipers. To obtuse thick brains like you it is all the same, but it is not, go get an education." Laila sounded angry. "Do you know how you are known to my children at home? ….. They call you Mr. Grouchy Bouchy". That is when James noticed Frakash and became angrier. "I am certain, that it is you who brought this terrorist into our office". Laila noticed Frakash as well and was surprised to see him standing in front of her, but she was too busy yelling at James. "You dim-witted toad, that is not a terrorist, that is my garden gnome". James retorted back in complete disbelief: "A garden gnome! look at him, he has a long beard and is wearing a turban, he must be a Bin Laden follower, he is here to corrupt the corporate culture of our democratic country from the inside. People like you are so broadminded that you are not able to tell the difference between right and wrong". Once more, Frakash didn't understand what Laila and James were talking about, but looking at James' shirtless body he had a suspicion that it had something to do with him stealing his t-shirt. Frakash stood on a nearby desk and cleared his throat "Please stop yelling. I am sorry I stole your t-shirt. I am sorry I tied you up in the washroom. I don't understand the things that you said about me, but I am just a garden gnome who is tired of living in fairy tale land. Once I got a taste of the brainy radiance of your office I wanted to become a computer programmer same as you. None of this is Laila's fault, she didn't even know that I was here, please take your t-shirt back". James took his shirt back and grumbled while walking away.

It took Laila ten minutes to stop shaking. Frakash calmed her down by showing her his sighing method. Twenty long exhales later, Laila composed herself, looked at Frakash intensely: "We need to have a serious talk, woman to garden gnome". Frakash heard Laila's children dreading a serious talk with their mom in the past. "Why didn't you tell me that you wanted to become a computer programmer? I would have arranged for you to come to the office and helped you figure things out.". Frakash answered sheepishly: "I thought that you would laugh at me, besides, you never talk with me in the garden, so how do you expect me to walk up to you and ask for a favor". Laila knew that Frakash made a valid point. "Well!" Laila paused thinking of a delicate way to say what she was thinking: "Until today, I assumed that your were deaf, mute and static, it never occurred to me to try to talk with you, had you started by saying a simple ehm!, it would have evaporated the barrier separating our two worlds". Frakash was puzzled: "Static! Who do you think makes your garden flourish every spring?", His voice conveyed a touch of hurt. "I

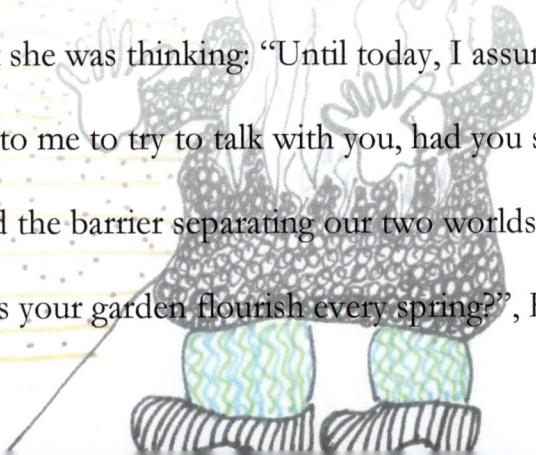

thought that it was my husband that worked in the garden" came the reply. Frakash threw his arms into the air and shrugged his shoulders in disbelief, "your garden flourishes despite your husband, not because of him.", was Frakash's retort. Laila felt an uneasy sensation in her stomach. The grumbling from her intestines made her quickly change the subject: "Tell me how you spent the day at the office? And are you by any chance behind the shrub design I have been hearing about?", Laila's voice became softer. Frakash recounted to Laila his day. He couldn't contain his surprise when he found out that the grey dragon was something called a printer and that the vampire and the werewolf were just a stapler and a pair of scissors. Finally, the monkeys that attacked him next to the plants were stuffed toys that a geekmeister named Tatiana keeps hanging in the potted plants to raise awareness to the plight of the chimpanzees in Africa.

That evening, Laila promised Frakash that she would take him to her office everyday to teach him how to develop his logical muscles. In exchange, he promised her that anytime she picked up a doughnut, he would, rescue the sugary delight and eat it.

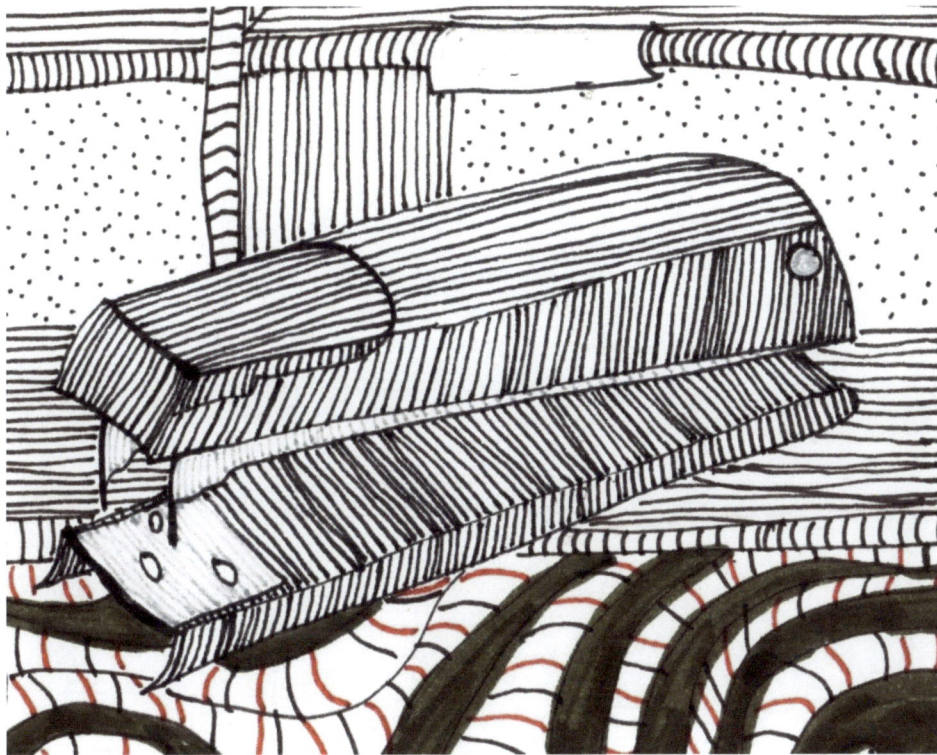

www.ingramcontent.com/pod-product-compliance
Lightning Source LLC
Chambersburg PA
CBHW041429090426
42741CB00003B/95